This book belongs to

....

The Sing Song and Other stories

How this collection works

This *Biff, Chip and Kipper* collection is one of a series of four books at **Read with Oxford Stage 2**. It is divided into two distinct halves.

The first half focuses on phonics, with two stories written in line with the phonics your child will have learned at school: *The Sing Song* and *The Red Coat*. The second half contains two stories that use everyday language: *Floppy and the Bone* and *Missing!* These stories help to broaden your child's wider reading experience. There are also fun activities to enjoy throughout the book.

How to use this book

Find a time to read with your child when they are not too tired and are happy to concentrate for about ten to fifteen minutes. Reading at this stage should be a shared and enjoyable experience. It is best to choose just one story for each session.

There are tips for each part of the book to help you make the most of the stories and activities. The tips for reading on pages 6 and 28 show you how to introduce your child to the phonics stories.

The tips for reading on pages 50 and 72 explain how you can best approach reading the stories that use a wider vocabulary. At the end of each of the four stories you will find four 'Talk about the story' questions. These will help your child to think about what they have read, and to relate the story to their own experiences. The questions are followed by a fun activity.

Enjoy sharing the stories!

Authors and illustrators

The Sing Song written by Roderick Hunt, illustrated by Nick Schon
The Red Coat written by Roderick Hunt, illustrated by Nick Schon
Floppy and the Bone written by Cynthia Rider, illustrated by Alex Brychta
Missing! written by Roderick Hunt, illustrated by Alex Brychta

OXFORD
UNIVERSITY PRESS

Great Clarendon Street, Oxford, OX2 6DP, United Kingdom

Oxford University Press is a department of the University
of Oxford. It furthers the University's objective of excellence
in research, scholarship, and education by publishing
worldwide. Oxford is a registered trade mark of Oxford
University Press in the UK and in certain other countries

The Red Coat, *The Sing Song*, *Missing!* text © Roderick Hunt 2006, 2007
Floppy and the Bone text © Cynthia Rider 2005

Floppy and the Bone, *Missing!* illustrations © Alex Brychta 2005, 2006
The Sing Song, *The Red Coat* illustrations © Alex Brychta and Nick Schon 2007

The characters in this work are the original creation of Roderick Hunt
and Alex Brychta who retain copyright in the characters

The moral rights of the authors have been asserted

Floppy and the Bone first published in 2005
Missing! first published in 2006
The Sing Song, *The Red Coat* first published in 2007

This Edition first published in 2018

British Library Cataloguing in Publication Data
Data available

ISBN: 978-0-19-276421-8

10 9 8 7 6 5 4 3 2

Paper used in the production of this book is a natural, recyclable product
made from wood grown in sustainable forests. The manufacturing process
conforms to the environmental regulations of the country of origin.

Printed in China

Acknowledgements

Series Editors: Annemarie Young and Kate Ruttle

Contents

OXFORD
UNIVERSITY PRESS

Phonics

Tips for reading *The Sing Song*

Children learn best when reading is relaxed and enjoyable.

- Talk about the title and the picture on page 7, and read the speech bubble at the bottom of that page.

- Identify the letter pattern *ng* in the title and talk about the sound it makes when you read it.

- Look at the *ng* and *ck* words on page 8. Say the sounds in each word and then say the word (e.g. *s-i-ng, sing; sh-o-ck, shock*).

- Read the story together then find the words with *ng* and *ck* in them.

- Talk about the story and do the fun activity on page 26.

Children enjoy re-reading stories and this helps to build their confidence.

Have fun!

After you have read the story, find the ten musical notes in the pictures. ♩ ♫

The main sound practised in this story is 'ng' as in *sang*. The other sound practised is 'ck' as in *rock*.

 For more activities, free eBooks and practical advice to help your child progress with reading visit **oxfordowl.co.uk**

The Sing Song

Who will win the sing song?

Say the sounds and read these words.

si**ng**   so**ng**

di**ng**   lo**ng**

alo**ng**   sa**ng**

ro**ck**   sho**ck**

"It is a Sing Song," said Dad.

"Let's go to the Sing Song,"
said Dad.

We can sing
a song.

"Yes, let's go along to it," said Mum.

They went to the Sing Song.

They met Wilf and Wilma.

Wilf and Wilma sang a song.
They had fun singing it.

Kipper had a song to sing.

Mum sang it with him.

Biff and Chip sang a song.

Such a sad song.

It was a sad song.

Dad sang a song.

He is cool.

It went on and on.

Dad sang and sang.

Dad won the Sing Song.

Talk about the story

Who did the family meet at the Sing Song?

What song did Kipper sing?

Why were Biff and Chip surprised that Dad won?

What do you like to sing?

Spot the difference

Find the five differences in the two pictures of Dad.

Tips for reading *The Red Coat*

Children learn best when reading is relaxed and enjoyable.

- Talk about the title and the picture on page 29, and read the speech bubble at the bottom of that page.

- Identify the letter pattern *oa* in the title and talk about the sound it makes when you read it.

- Look at the *oa* and *ng* words on page 30. Say the sounds in each word and then say the word (e.g. *s-oa-p*, *soap*).

- Read the story together, then find the words with *oa* in them.

- Talk about the story and do the fun activity on page 48.

Children enjoy re-reading stories and this helps to build their confidence.

Have fun!

After you have read the story, find eight stars in the pictures.

The main sound practised in this story is 'oa' as in *coat*.

For more activities, free eBooks and practical advice to help your child progress with reading visit **oxfordowl.co.uk**

The Red Coat

Chip needs a red coat.

Say the sounds and read these words.

c**oa**t	s**oa**p
s**oa**k	f**oa**m
ki**ng**	po**ng**s

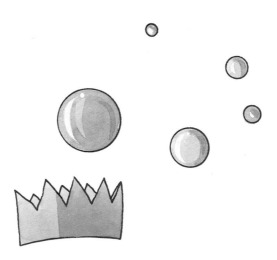

Chip was a king.

I am King Chip.

"I am a king," Chip said
to Mum.

"I need a king's coat,"
he said.

A red coat.

Mum took Chip to a shop.

Chip put on a red coat.

The coat had an odd smell.

It pongs.

"Yuk. It smells odd,"
said Chip.

Chip put the coat in the tub.

"It can soak in the tub,"
he said.

What a lot of foam.

Dad had a load of washing.

40

Chip put the coat in.

Dad's washing was red.

Look at the red foam.

"Look at my washing,"
said Dad.

It's all red.

Chip was upset.

"But look at the coat," said Mum.

"He is the red king,"
said Mum.

Talk about the story

Why did Chip want a red coat?

What was wrong with the coat?

Why did Dad's washing turn red?

What do you like dressing up as?

Spot the difference

Find the five differences in the two pictures of Chip.

Stories for Wider Reading

Tips for reading the stories together

These two stories use simple everyday language. You can help your child to read any more challenging words in the context of the story. Children enjoy re-reading stories and this helps to build their confidence and their vocabulary.

Tips for reading *Floppy and the Bone*

- Talk about the title and the speech bubble on page 51, and look through the pictures so that your child can see what the story is about.
- Read the story together, encouraging your child to read as much as they can with you.
- Give lots of praise as your child reads with you, and help them when necessary.
- If your child gets stuck on a word that is easily decodable, encourage them to say the sounds and then blend them together to read the word. Read the whole sentence again. Focus on the meaning. If the word is not decodable, or is still too tricky, just read the word for them and move on.
- When you've finished reading the story, talk about it with your child, using the 'Talk about the story' questions at the end.
- Do the activity on page 70.
- Re-read the story later, again encouraging your child to read as much of it as they can.

After you have read the story, find the butterfly hidden in every picture.

Have fun!

This story includes these useful common words:

said   the   went   saw

For more activities, free eBooks and practical advice to help your child progress with reading visit **oxfordowl.co.uk**

Floppy and the Bone

Floppy wanted the big bone.

Floppy saw a big bone.

"I want that bone,"
said Floppy.

He got the bone!

"Stop! Stop!" said Biff.

"Drop the bone!" said Chip.

But Floppy did not stop,
and he did not drop the bone!

He ran up the hill.

He ran into a wood...

and onto a bridge...
and he stopped!

Floppy looked down.

He saw a dog in the water.

The dog had a big bone.

Floppy wanted that bone, too.

Grrrrrrrr!
went Floppy.

SPLASH! went the bone.
SPLASH! went Floppy.

"Oh no!" said Floppy.
"The dog I saw was me!"

Talk about the story

Why do you think Floppy took the bone?

What did Floppy see in the water? Did he think it was a real dog?

Do you think Floppy was a sensible dog in this story?

Have you ever wanted something as much as Floppy wanted his bone?

Picture puzzle

How many things can you find beginning with the same sound as the 'b' in ball?

Tips for reading *Missing!*

- Talk about the title and the speech bubble on page 73, and look through the pictures so that your child can see what the story is about.

- Read the story together, encouraging your child to read as much as they can with you.

- Give lots of praise as your child reads with you, and help them when necessary.

- If your child gets stuck on a word that is easily decodable, encourage them to say the sounds and then blend them together to read the word. Read the whole sentence again. Focus on the meaning. If the word is not decodable, or is still too tricky, just read the word for them and move on.

- Read the whole sentence again. Focus on the meaning.

- When you've finished reading the story, talk about it with your child, using the 'Talk about the story' questions at the end.

- Do the activity on pages 92.

- Re-read the story later, again encouraging your child to read as much of it as they can.

Have fun!

Find the 10 nuts hidden in the pictures.
There are 2 of each of these.

This story includes these useful common words:

said   was   saw   looked

For more activities, free eBooks and practical advice to help your child progress with reading visit **oxfordowl.co.uk**

Missing!

Jaws is missing!

Nadim had a hamster.
He called it Jaws.

"Jaws is a funny name for
a hamster," said Biff.

Nadim put Jaws in his cage, but
he forgot to shut the cage door.

Jaws got out of the cage
and ran off.

Nadim saw the cage was open.
"Oh no!" he said.

Nadim was upset.

"Jaws has run off," said Nadim.

"We can look for him," said Biff.
They looked and looked.

Biff looked under the sink.
Chip looked in the fridge.

Nadim looked under the
cupboard.

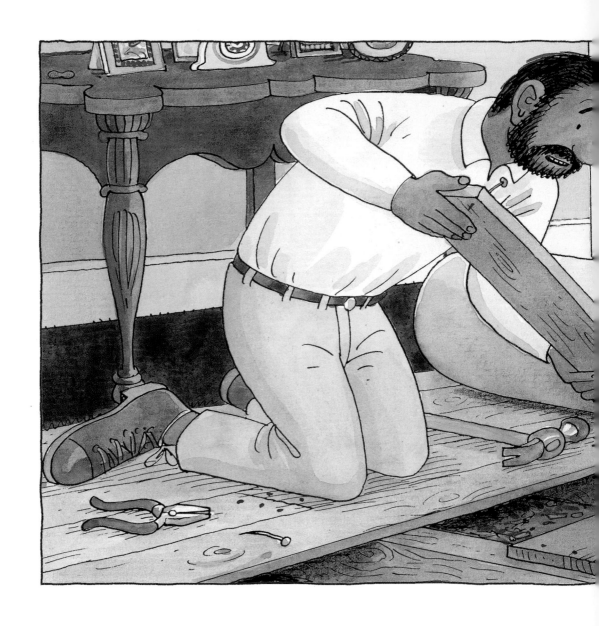

Nadim's dad looked under
the floor.

"Is Jaws down here?" he said.

Then Chip had an idea.
"Let's get Floppy. He can
help us."

Sniff, sniff, went Floppy.

Sniff, sniff! SNIFF! SNIFF!
"Look in there," said Chip.

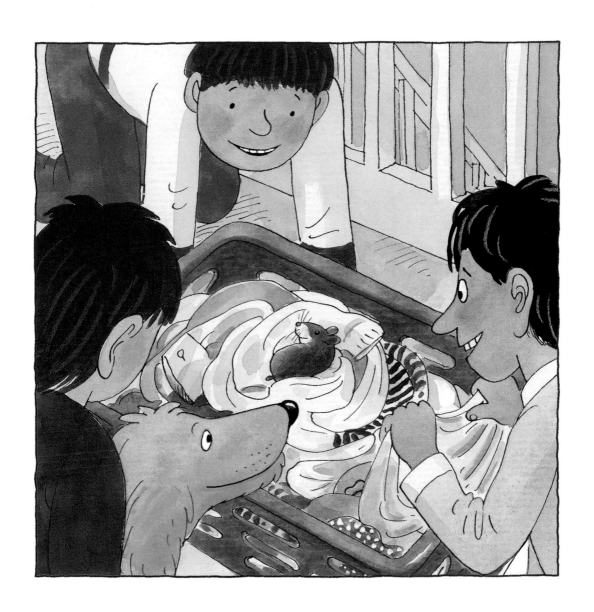

Jaws was in the clothes basket.
He had made a nest.

"Look!" said Nadim. "You can see why I called him Jaws."

Talk about the story

Why is the hamster called Jaws?

Why was Nadim upset when he found that Jaws had run away?

Where did the children and Dad look for Jaws?

What would you do if you lost your pet?

Odd one out

Which two things don't begin with the same sound as the 'h' at the beginning of 'hamster'?

Remembering the stories together

Encourage your child to remember and retell the stories in this book. You could ask questions like these:

- Who are the characters in the story?
- What happens at the beginning of the story?

- What happens next?
- How does the story end?
- What was your favourite part of the story? Why?

Story prompts

When talking to your child about the stories, you could use these more detailed reminders to help them remember the exact sequence of events. Turn the statements below into questions, so that your child can give you the answers. For example, *Where are Mum and Dad taking the children? Who does Mum sing with?* And so on …

The Sing Song

- Mum and Dad take the children to the singing competition.
- Wilf and Wilma have fun singing a song.
- Mum sings a song with Kipper.

- Biff and Chip sing a sad song.
- Dad sings a rock song and goes on and on.
- Dad wins the singing competition.

The Red Coat

- Chip is dressing up as a king, but he needs a king's coat.
- Mum takes Chip to a charity shop to find a king's coat.
- He puts on a red coat, but it has an odd smell and is too big.

- Chip puts the coat in the washing machine with Dad's washing.
- The coat turns the washing red, but the coat is now the right size.
- Chip is now the red king!

Floppy and the Bone

- Floppy sees another dog's bone and wants it!

- He takes the bone and runs off as fast as he can.

- The children chase him across the park to the river.

- Floppy sees his reflection in the water.

- He sees the reflection of his bone and wants it.

- He tries to get the other bone and falls into the water.

Missing!

- Nadim has a hamster called Jaws.

- Nadim forgets to shut the cage door and Jaws escapes!

- Biff, Chip and Nadim look everywhere for Jaws.

- Nadim's dad even looks under the floorboards.

- Then Floppy finds Jaws in the clothes basket.

- Nadim's T-shirt has been nibbled by Jaws.

You could now encourage your child to create a 'story map' of each story, drawing and colouring all the key parts of them. This will help them to identify the main elements of the stories and learn to create their own stories.